get

lost

GET LOST

AN A→Z OF MAZES

by ian

apple

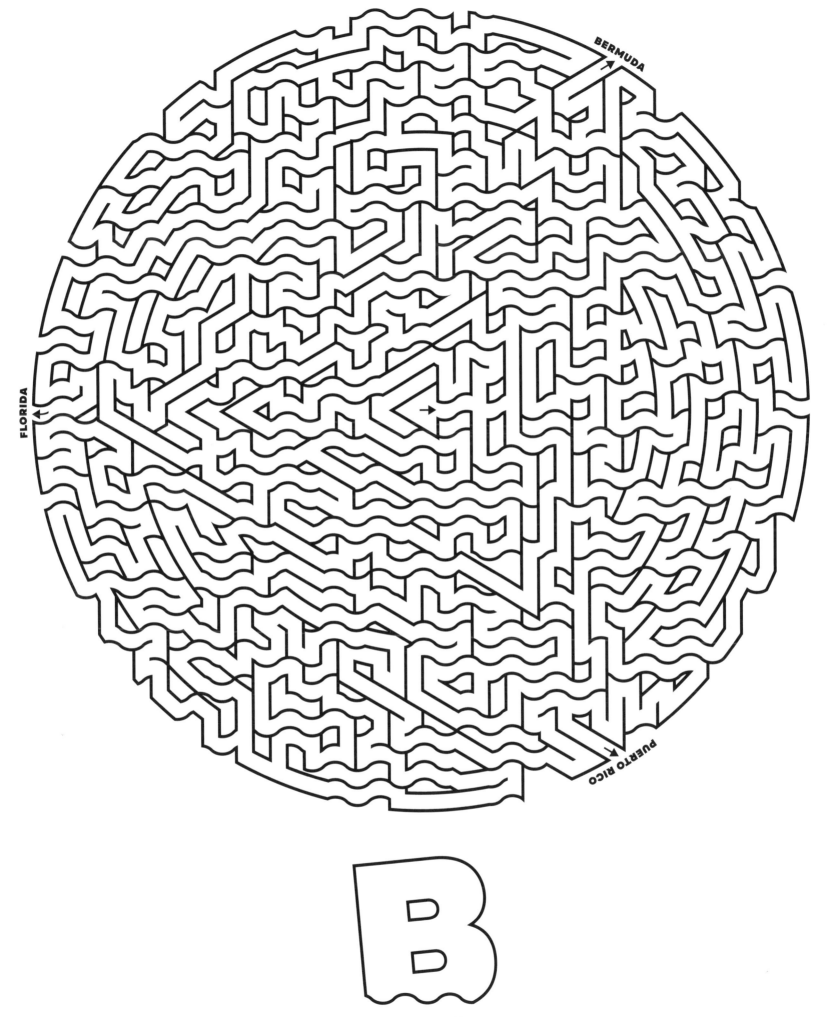

B

Bermuda Triangle

carpet weaving

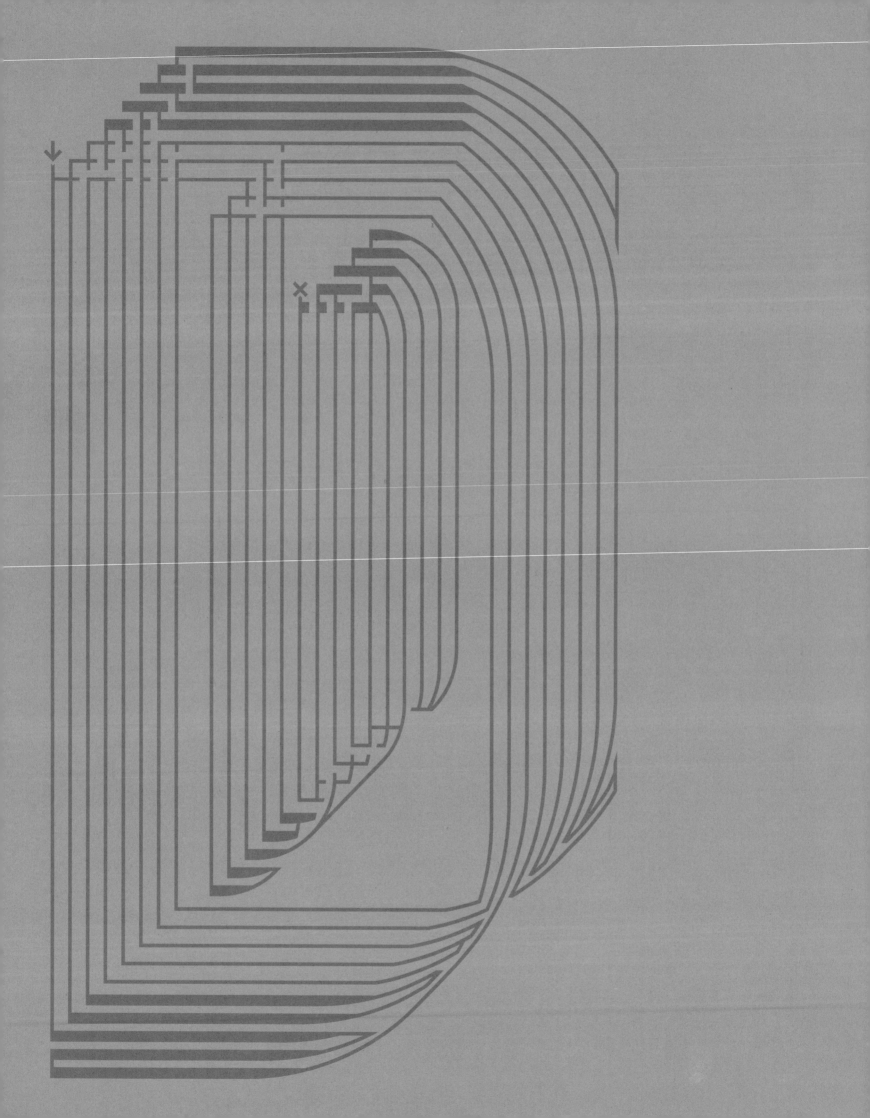

draw a line in the sand

exit strategy

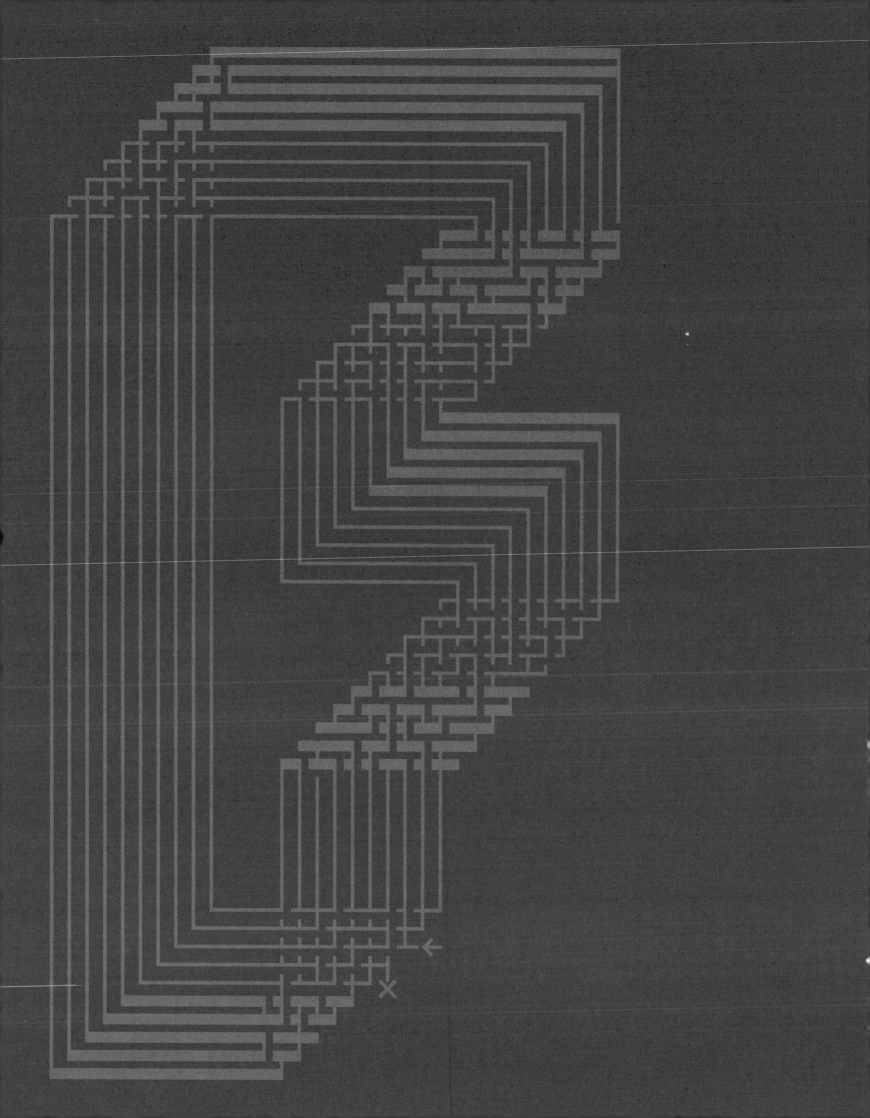

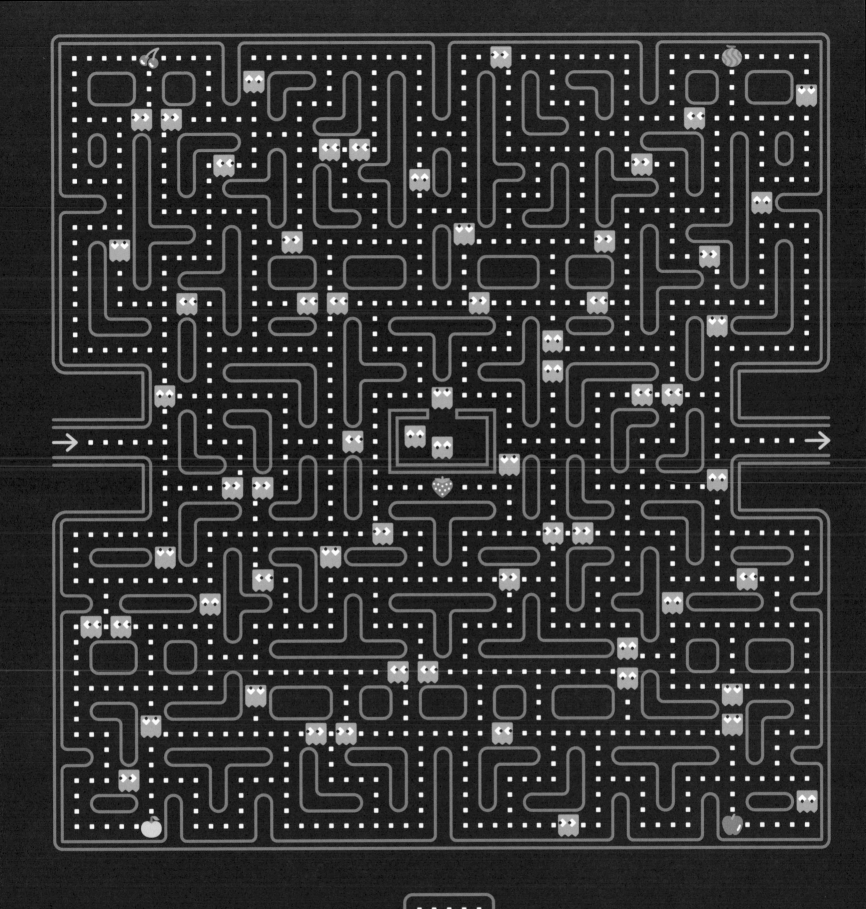

five a day*

*collect all five

global warming

happily ever after

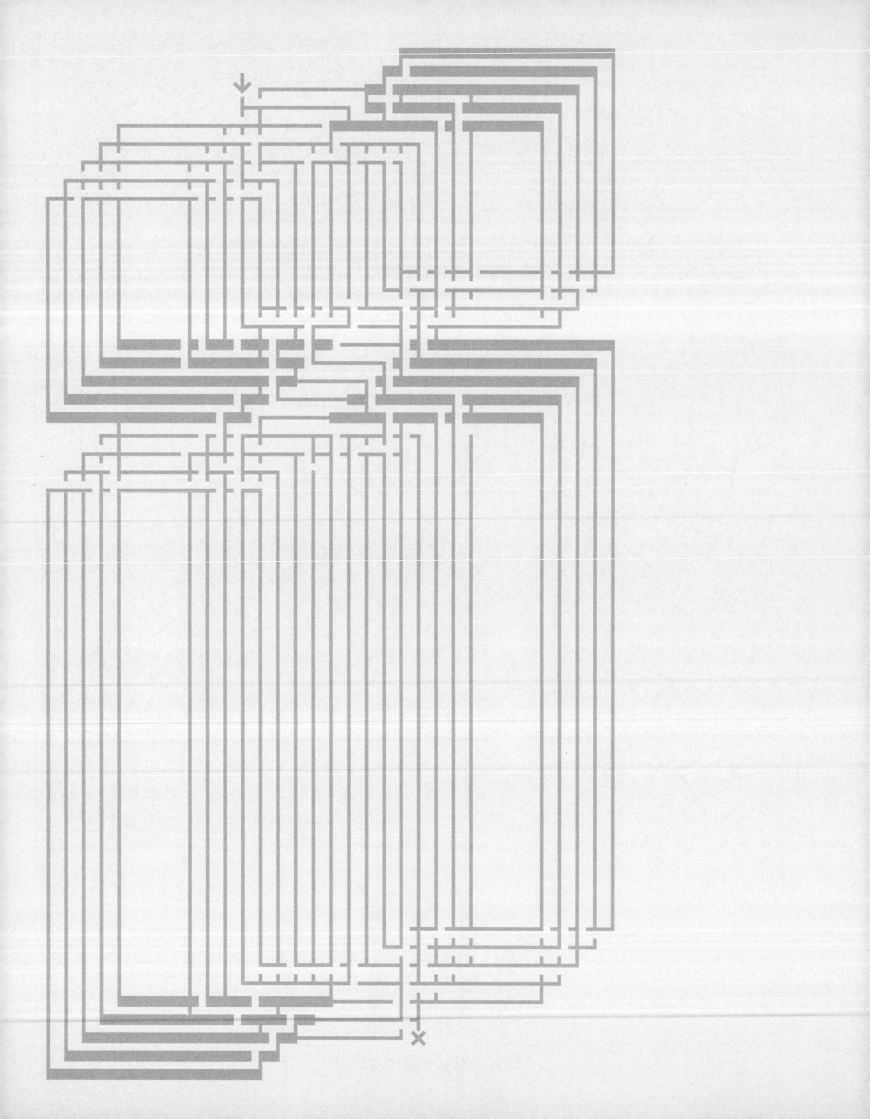

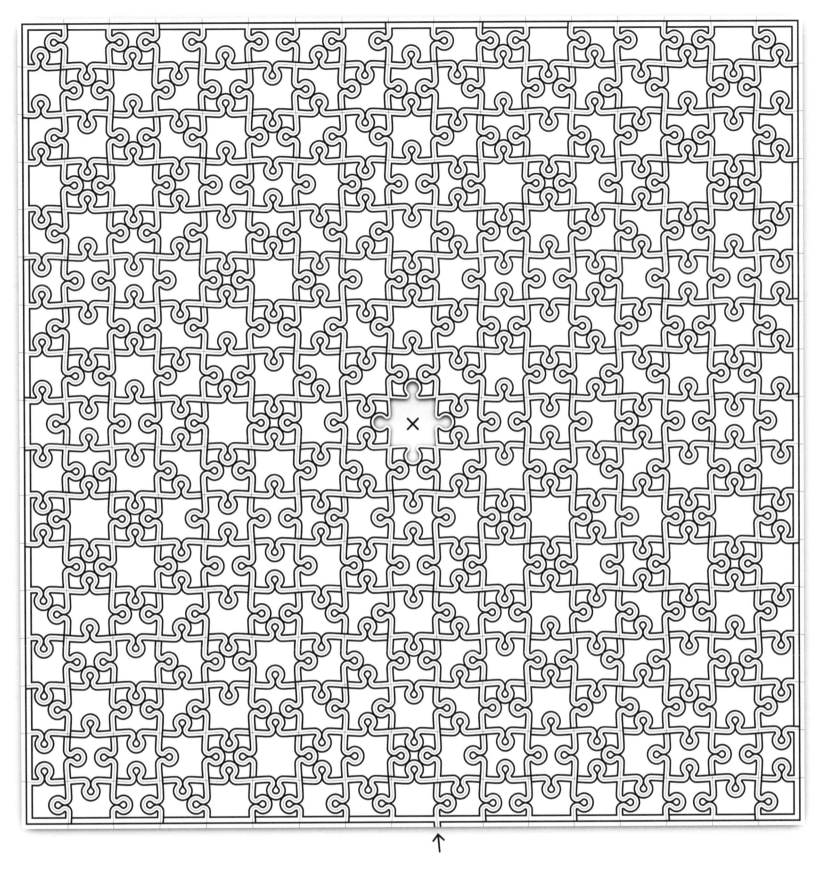

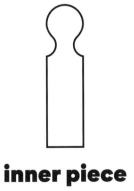

inner piece

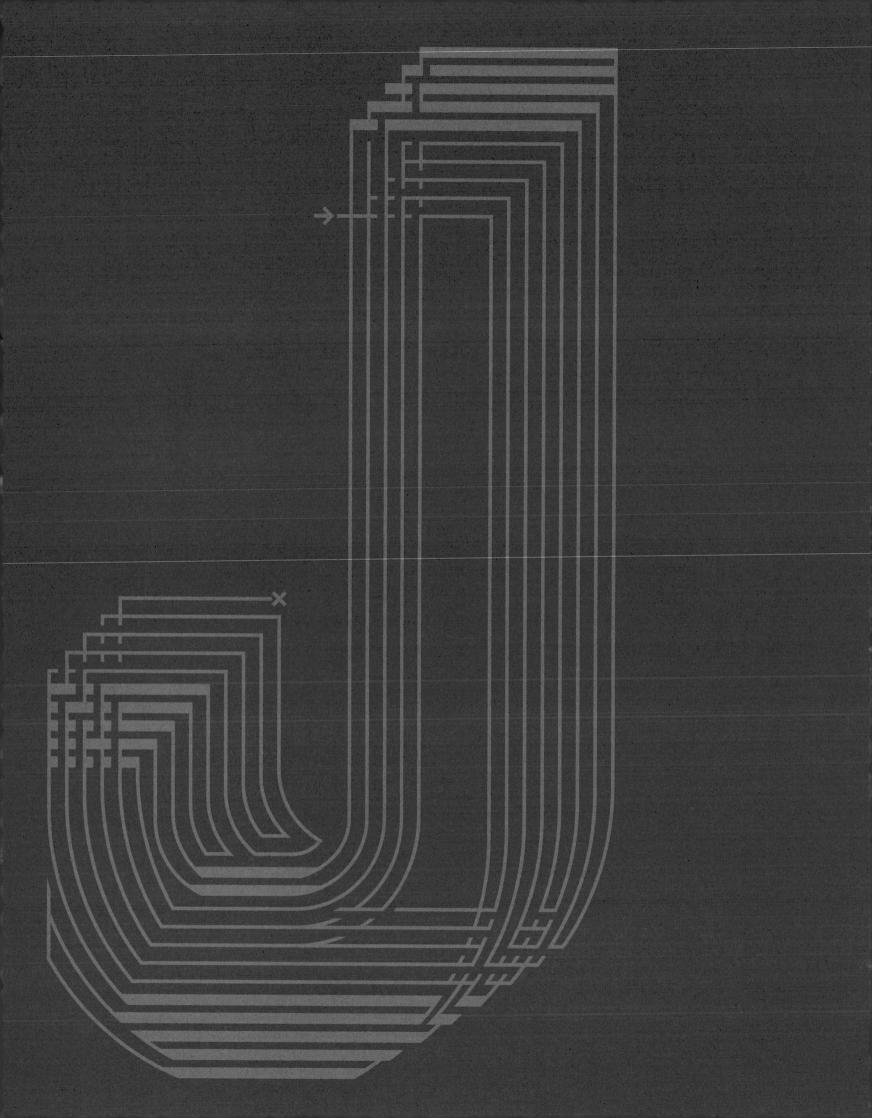

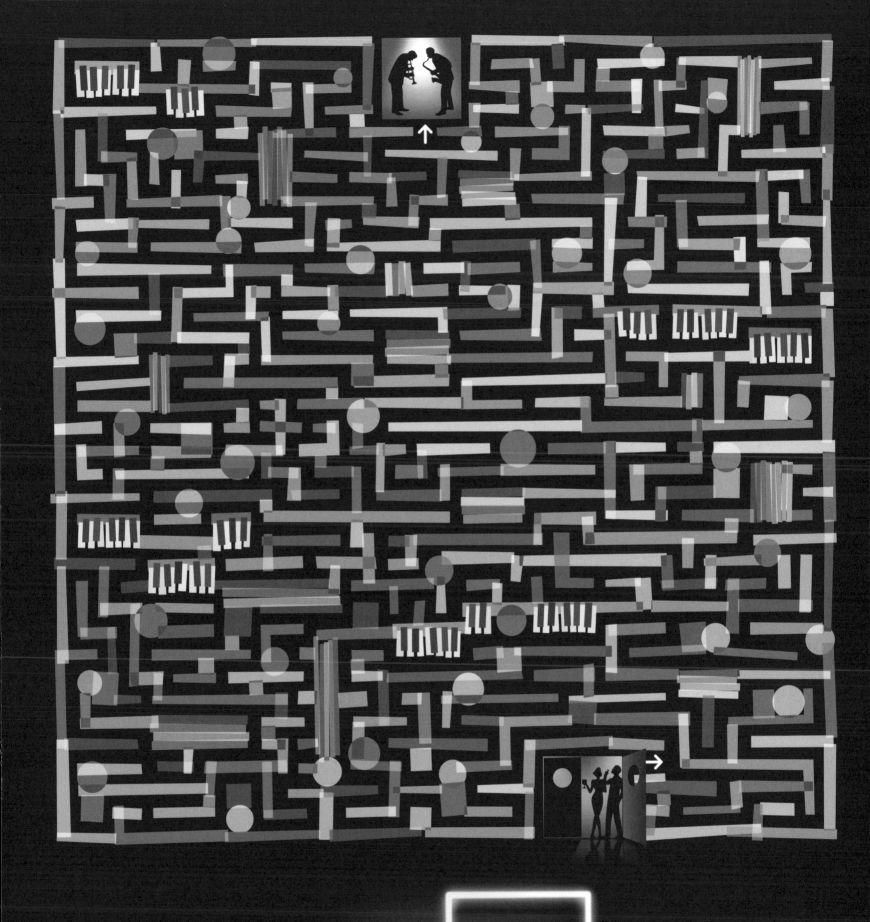

jazz club

knitting needles

lost in music

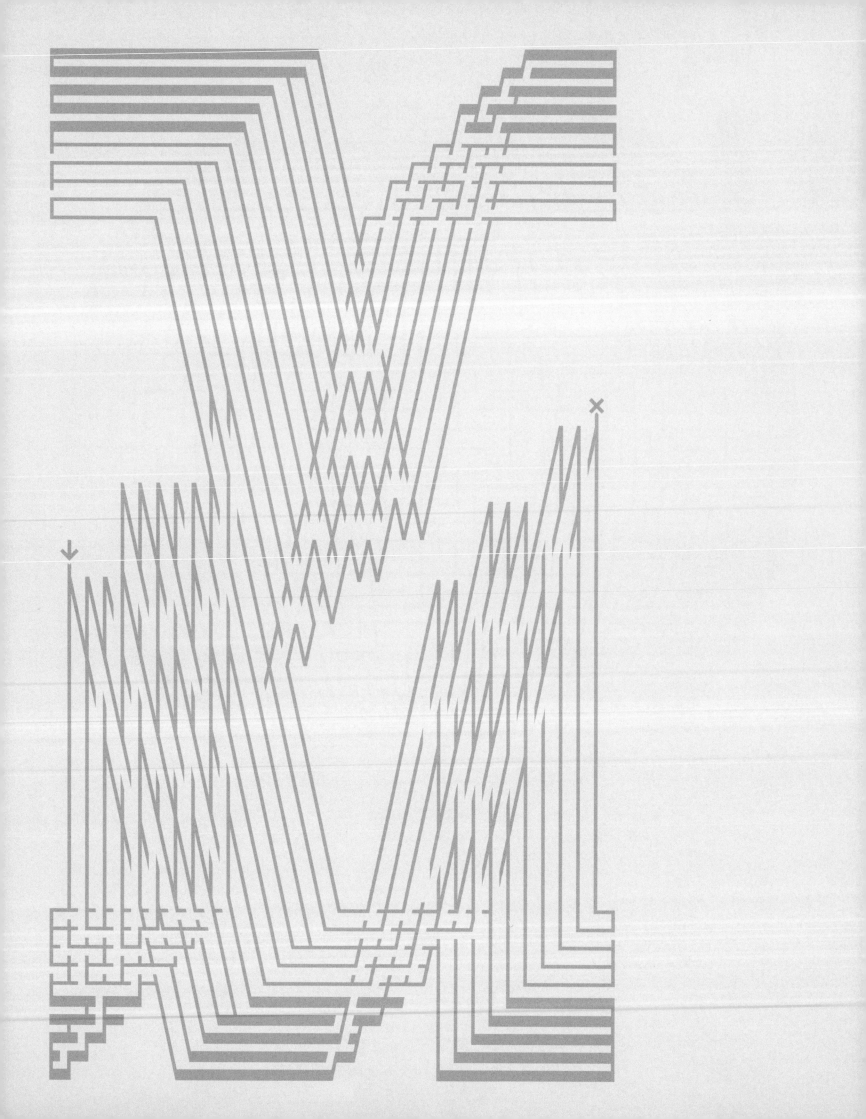

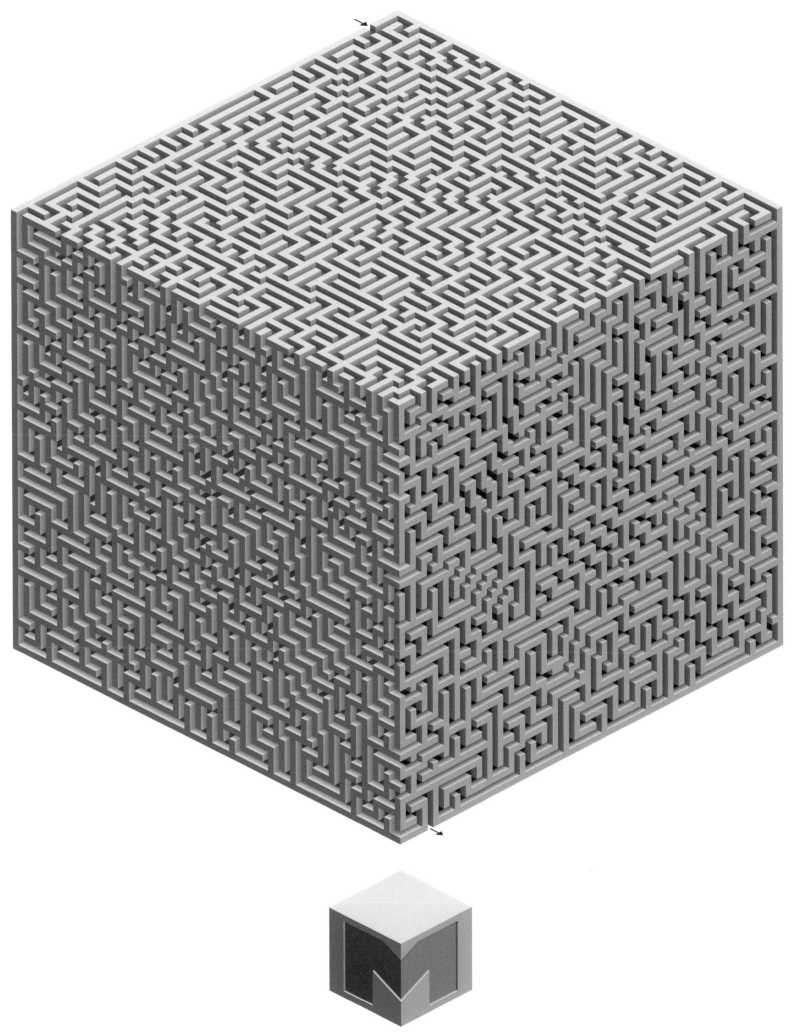

mental block

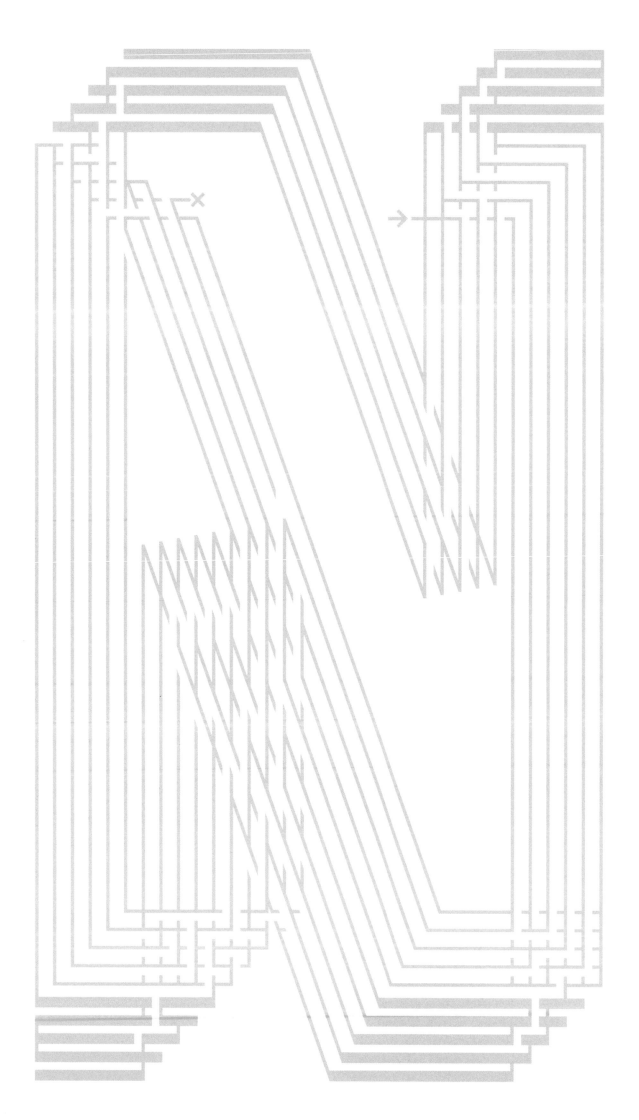

nature trail

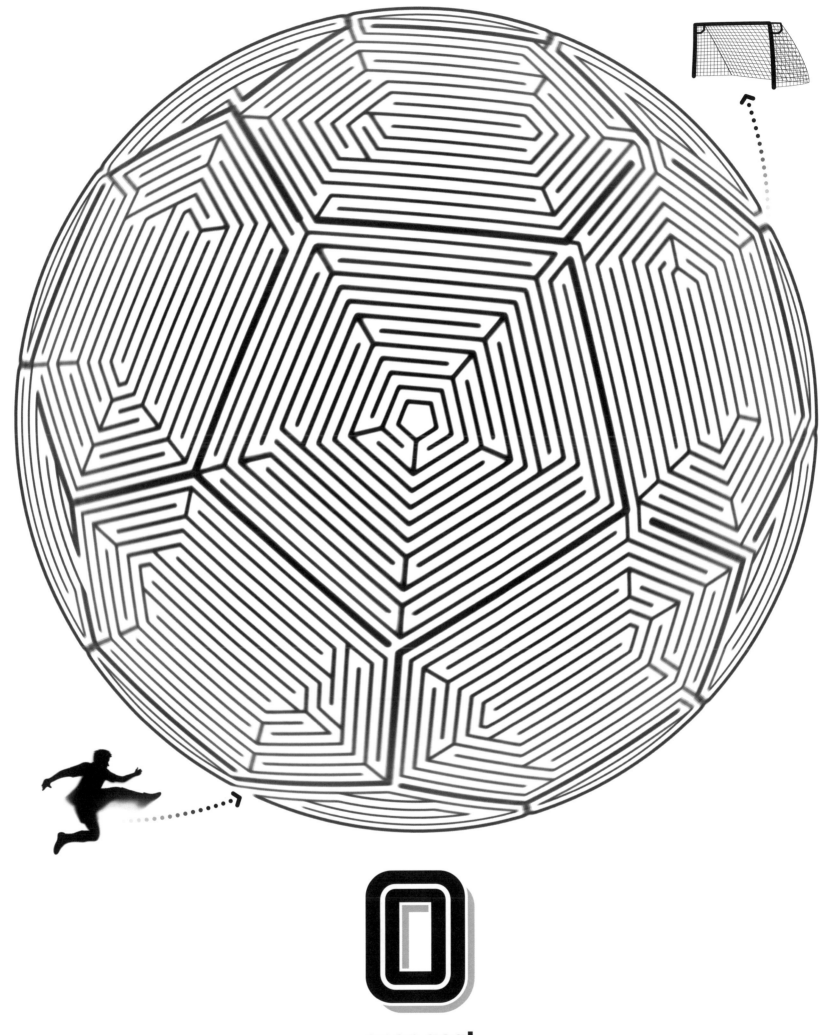

open goal

pyramid scheme

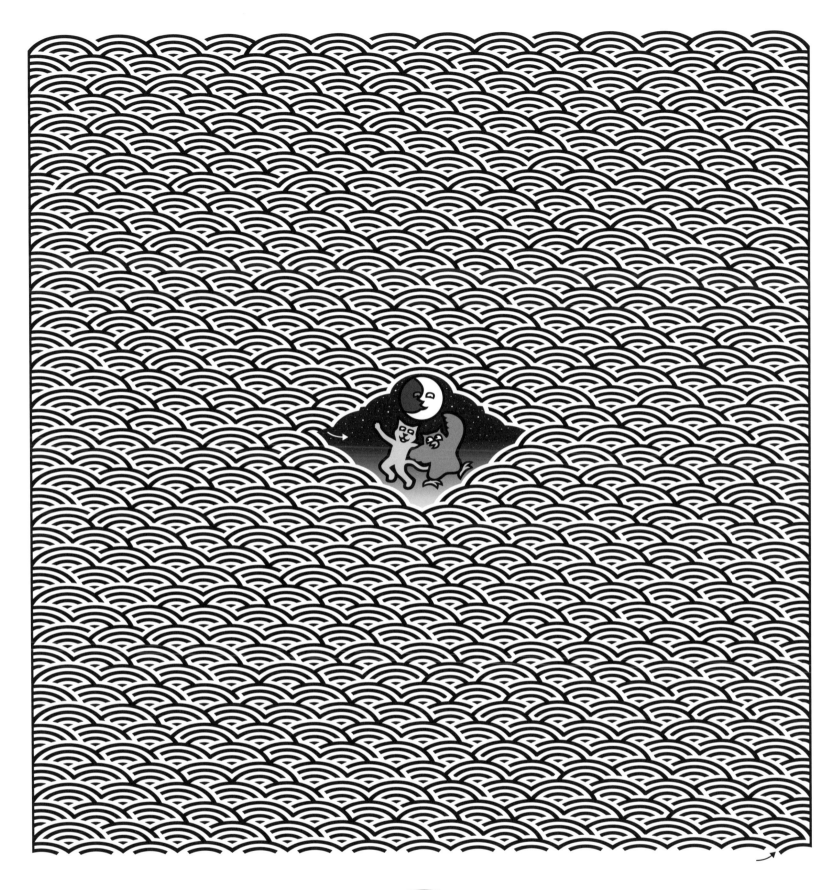

quality time

rule of six[*]

stargazing

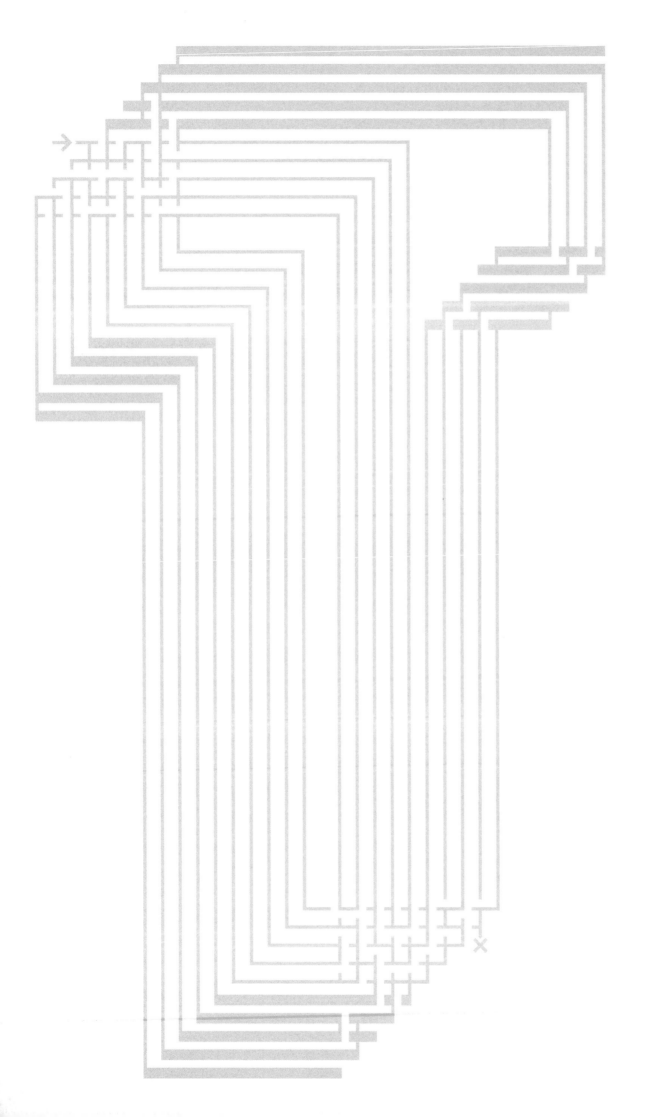

too much of a good thing *

up the junction

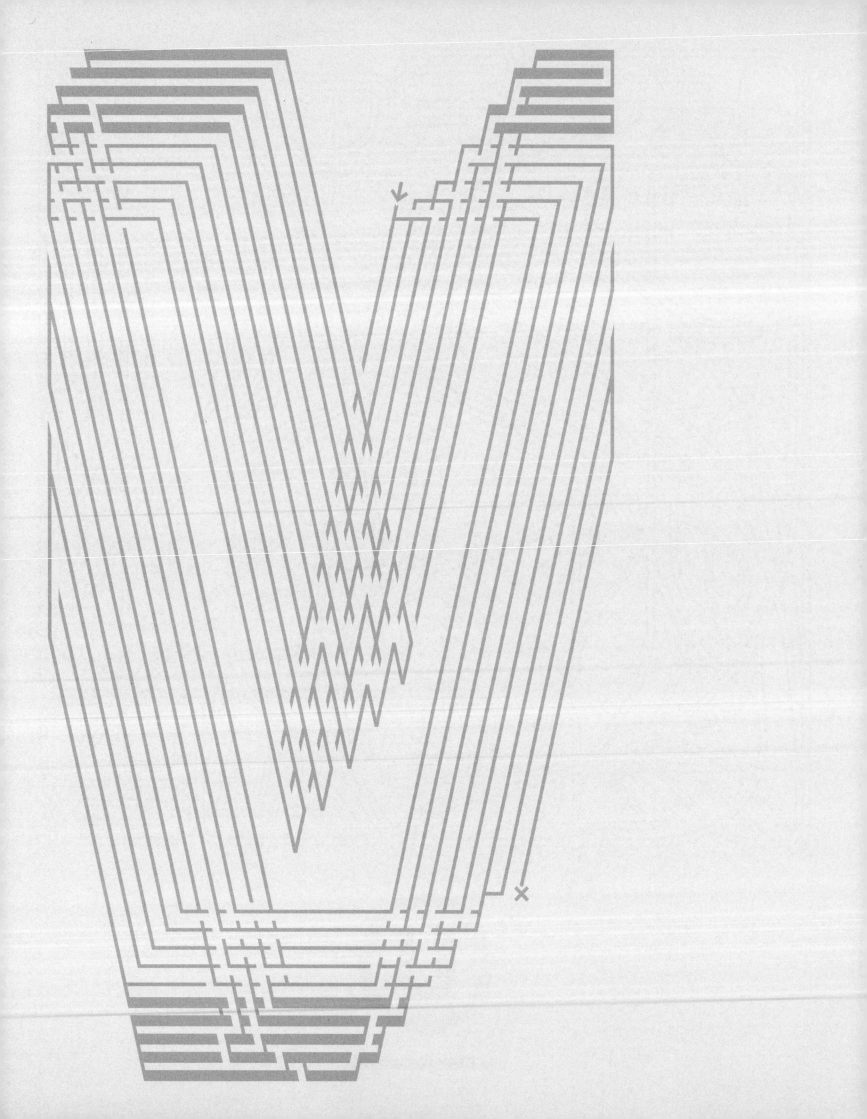

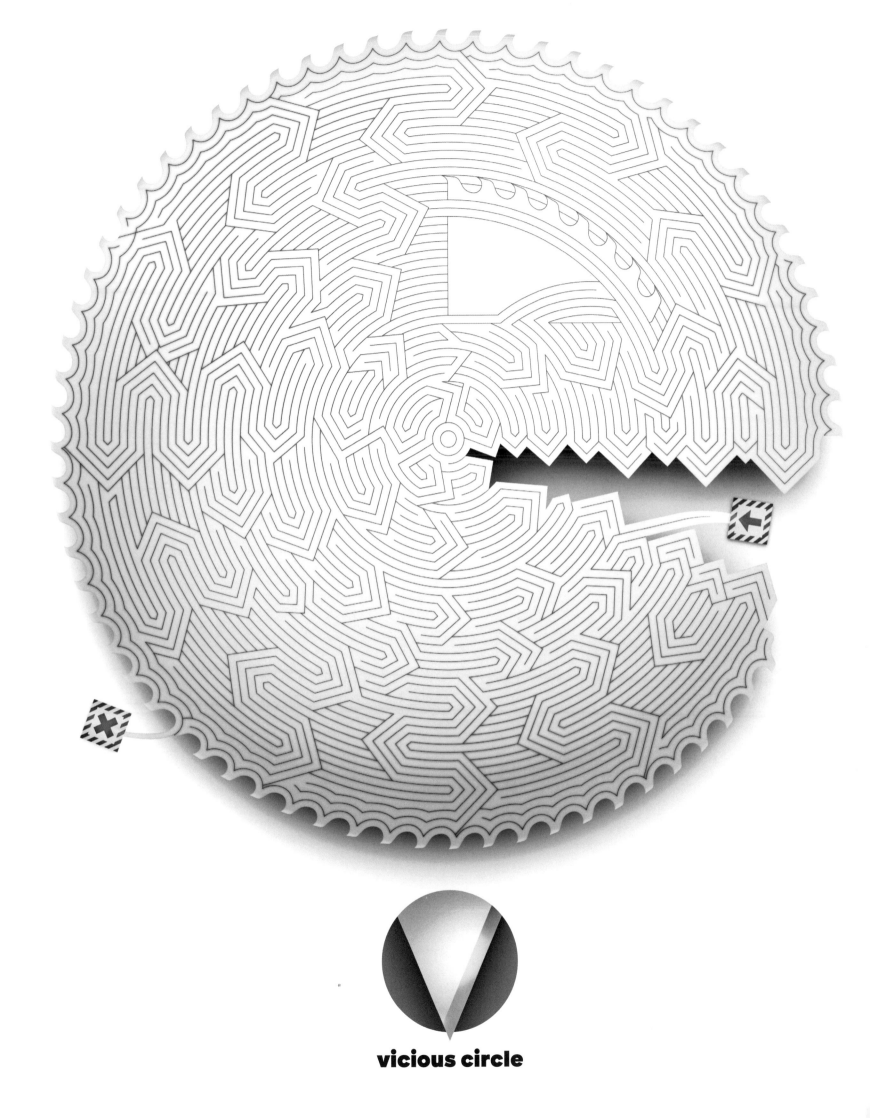

vicious circle

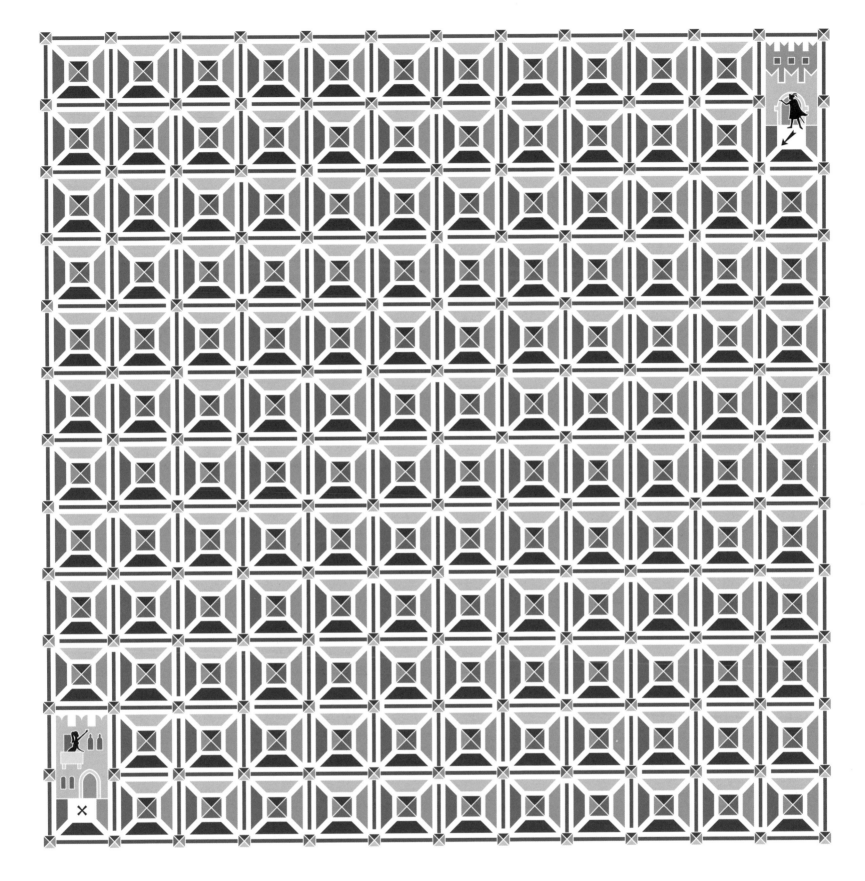

wherefore art thou?

xbox

Y

you know who

z

zebra crossing

First published in 2021 by E&P
142 Newbridge Road · Bath · BA1 3LD · UK
hello@eandp.co.uk · www.eandp.co.uk

Are you still lost?

If finding a way through the mazes remains elusive then, for a small charitable donation, a downloadable pdf of the routes is available.

Please make a suggested donation of £5 or more to the Centre for Alternative Technology at cat.org.uk/donate. For 'How did you find out about us?' select 'other' and write 'Get Lost book'.

Then forward the email receipt from your donation to getlost@solution4u.com and a link to download the pdf will be sent to you.

Centre for Alternative Technology
Canolfan y Dechnoleg Amgen

All is not lost

The world's eco-system is in the balance. The Centre for Alternative Technology are inspiring and informing us about how we can respond to this climate and biodiversity emergency.

CAT aims to help us reduce greenhouse gas emissions, adapt to climate impacts, restore biodiversity, improve public health, reduce fuel and food poverty, create jobs and enhance well-being. Together we can achieve a sustainable future for all humanity as part of a thriving natural world.

ISBN 9781399902816

British Library cataloguing-in-publication data: a catalogue record for this book is available from the British Library.

Printed in the Czech Republic by Akcent Media: pages on Munken Polar Rough (FSC certified); cover on Europapier IQ Print (PEFC and EU Ecolabel certified)

FSC
www.fsc.org

MIX
Paper from responsible sources
FSC® C137584

I'd be lost without you

Love and hugs to Lisa and Harry and Tom.

Ian would like to thank the many people who have either inspired, intervened, tolerated or once held a door open for him. They include: Howel & Edna, Jim Porteous, Emma Moore/Agency 74, Dom Phillips/New City Press, Ken Garland, Paul Stiff, Peter Barrett, Arthur op den Brouw, Martin Cottingham/Soil Association, and John Sansom.

LOVE PAPER

www.lovepaper.org